PENGUIN BOOKS

CW00501728

THE
CURLY PYJAMA
LETTERS

Michael Leunig has been drawing
and writing for Australian newspapers since 1965. He was born
in Melbourne and now lives on
a farm in north-eastern Victoria.
The Curly Pyjama Letters first
appeared as occasional pieces in
the Melbourne *Age*.

Also by Michael Leunig

The Penguin Leunig
The Second Leunig
The Bedtime Leunig
A Bag of Roosters
Ramming the Shears
The Travelling Leunig
A Common Prayer
The Prayer Tree
Common Prayer Collection
Introspective
A Common Philosophy
Everyday Devils and Angels
A Bunch of Poesy
You and Me
Short Notes from the Long History of Happiness
Why Dogs Sniff Each Other's Tails
Goatperson
The Stick
Poems: 1972–2002
Strange Creature
Wild Figments
A New Penguin Leunig

MICHAEL LEUNIG

THE
CURLY PYJAMA
LETTERS

PENGUIN BOOKS

PENGUIN BOOKS

UK | USA | Canada | Ireland | Australia
India | New Zealand | South Africa | China

Penguin Books is part of the Penguin Random House group of companies
whose addresses can be found at global.penguinrandomhouse.com

Penguin
Random House
Australia

First published by Penguin Books Australia Ltd, 2001
This paperback edition published by Penguin Group (Australia), 2006

Design by George Dale © Penguin Group (Australia)
Typeset in Palatino light
Scanning and separations by Splitting Image P/L, Clayton, Victoria
Printed and bound in China

National Library of Australia
Cataloguing-in-Publication data:

Leunig, Michael, 1945– .
The curly pyjama letters.
Paperback ed.
ISBN: 978 0 14 300546 9 (pbk).
1. Caricatures and cartoons – Australia. 2. Australian wit and humor, pictorial. I. Title.

741.5994

penguin.com.au

to unusual friendships

The town of Curly Flat

Introduction

THE TWENTY-NINE LETTERS here published amount to a small fragment of the vast correspondence which is known to have taken place between lone voyager Vasco Pyjama and his friend and mentor Mr Curly of Curly Flat. How this handful of letters has come to light is something of a mystery, except to say that they simply 'appeared' as a small bundle tied up with a thin blue ribbon – the sort that can be found on a baby's bootie or bonnet.

Curiously they are not dated, and in the absence of an apparent chronology or thematic sequence (with the exception of some obvious pairings) they are presented in this volume in a 'whimsical/poetic' order sympathetic, it is hoped, to the spontaneous, meandering nature of the relationship which is evident between the correspondents.

Apart from what can be gleaned from the writing, precious little is known about the curriculum vitae of either Vasco Pyjama or Mr Curly. Rumours of sightings and snippets of heresay have come and gone over the years regarding past and present circumstances, but they all elude substantiation. Contradictory tales emerge and the image of the Curly–Pyjama world fades into the mist; the signal disappears and the mystery deepens. The truth could be that souls like Vasco and Curly are with us always, eternally present and reliably under our noses, it's just that we are unable to see them; we are blind to their realness, their openness, their sheer improbability and their noble innocence. Perhaps they become invisible when our gaze becomes too fierce, and then we declare that they are mystical, enigmatic and elusive. Yet they stand humbly and simply before us – at our feet while we search the clouds for their existence.

It is generally accepted, however, that Mr Curly still lives somewhere by the shores of Lake Lacuna near Curly Flat where, amongst other pursuits, he is actively and passionately absorbed in matters of horticulture, birdwatching, music and winemaking. His wines from the Curly Flat vineyard are legendary for the gentleness, cheerfulness and lyricism of their intoxication. Domestic contentment and ease with the natural world appear to be Mr Curly's major attrib- utes or achievements – but not at the expense of an

expressive and spirited personal style.

Vasco Pyjama probably started his life in Curly Flat, where the great friendship began, but his searching and restless nature has compelled him into his great voyage of discovery – the circumnavigation of his own world. In the company of his direction-finding duck (a sort of living compass which, according to Vasco, 'always points toward new joys'), he has left his home and wandered far and wide into his uncharted world,

Vasco Pyjama's perilous voyage through the dreaded
Strait of a Thousand Lighthouses.

risking, finding, enjoying and observing much. He is
clearly the more troubled and vulnerable of the two;
more easily shaken and bruised; more prone to
self-doubt, disillusionment or spiritual intoxication –
and perhaps possessed of a lonelier, more ecstatic
vision.

Despite their different natures, the two friends have
created a common language style – a shared personal
dialect which might be variously described as Naïve
Formal, Mock Victorian, Reserved Romantic or Quaint

Melodramatic. Were it a spoken language it would sound affected, perhaps, but in the written form it is clearly a language of unique personal protocol, as is often found in conversations between creative and intelligent minds in awe of life's complex grandeur, beauty and pathos. In the language of protocol much can be said and read between the lines, between the words; it serves well the discussion of philosophy which is both finely sensed and deeply felt, as is the

In Curly Flat unforeseen circumstances are celebrated ... accidents bring out the best in people.

case in the Curly–Pyjama correspondence. True formality allows for and provides great creative space and great lyrical acoustics.

Letters, of course, imply distance – often huge distance in space and time – and between separated dear friends there is often, in their mutual correspondence, an underlying yearning for each other's actual presence, an emotional undertone which flows from a thwarted passionate impulse to simply *be* with and hold the other in all their sensuality and truth. Such passion sometimes requires a certain linguistic bearing to make the heartache more bearable.

It is obvious to anyone but an emotional philistine that Curly and Vasco love each other and that, though they both enjoy their separate and differing lives, they also long for the day when they can be together again in peace and merriment on the sunny slopes overlooking the shores of Lake Lacuna. And of course the duck would be included. Perhaps they are there now, the three of them – reunited at Curly Flat. Nobody knows. Perhaps new facts will come to light, but for the moment all we have are these letters and the thin blue ribbon which held them together.

Michael Leunig

Dear Mr. Curly,

I have not written to you for quite some time, I suppose because there has been very little to report. My journey appears to have developed into a process of steady plodding which I rather like. When you plod, everything seems to take forever and forever is a lovely thing once you stop being scared of it.

Strange, how something that takes a lot of time can give a feeling that there _is_ a lot of time — and a lot of space and a good measure of ease. So onward I plod, through beautiful things and terrible things, too numerous to mention, with my duck

ahead of me and my gargling angel to
protect me from above. I am well and I
hope you are too.

    Best wishes; yours truly,

       Vasco Pyjama.

P.S. Is it "gargling" angel or "guardian" angel ?
  Somebody once suggested it should be
 "guardian" but I grew up believing it was
 "gargling"—"My gargling angel" and that's
 how I think of it. Oh well, whatever; it
 seems to care for me !

Dear Mr. Curly,
blessings and warm salutations — long
time no sea! Just a brief note to tell
you I am presently staying in a very
strange and wobbly place and in spite
of a shaky start, I am beginning to
enjoy myself. All varieties of wobbling seem
to abound here as a natural condition of
life. Wobbling, wiggling, waggling, wavering,
fluttering, fluctuating shimmering: all
actions, all thoughts, all feelings and all of
matter itself seem animated by these
qualities. Nothing is firm, nothing is solid;
and because there is no expectation of
firmness here, there seems to be no
problem with all this fluidity, in fact there

appear to be many pleasing and delightful outcomes. Surprisingly, life seems to proceed successfully enough and I am learning much about living with movement and the ever changing shape of large and small things. I still find it a bit difficult to write when the ground under my feet starts moving as it is doing right now. Perhaps the best way to deal with this particular situation is to bid you a fond adieu — after all, there comes a time to put down one's pen and to rest one's tongue. Adieu, adieu — with love,

Vasco Pyjama.

P.S. THE DUCK IS WELL.

12

Dear Vasco,
Summer is almost with us here in Curly
Flat and the season of the asparagus
is all but finished. Never have I enjoyed
such delicious asparagus curls as the ones
we harvested this spring. How remarkable
and odd that this delectable shoot, this
point of emergence into the rough, wild
world is so tender and full of goodness,
and how exploited and wounded it is
for these beautiful qualities.

How interesting Vasco, that growth
meets so much resistance, attracts
such brutality, its creations are so
constantly plundered — and yet it

persists and is tender — troubled
and tender! Growth is troubled
and tender. C'est la vie.

One more thing: asparagus certainly
is food for thought!

Protect yourself Vasco,
yours truly

Mr. Curly.
xxx

Dear Mr. Curly,

I am writing to tell you that I expect to be in Curly Flat for Christmas and look forward to seeing you. The duck is waddling wearily (but steadfastly) in a homeward direction and has got that faraway, forbearing look in its eye. Naturally I am following and if most things go well we should be moving along the shores of Lake Lacuna by christmas eve on the final stretch of our journey back to some peace and quiet.

The world through which we have been travelling seems to be in the grip of a particular madness. I can think of no other word for it but "mania", yet many other words are used; such are the many and varied faces of mania. It is called "passion". It is called "excitement." It is even called "celebration." And now whenever I hear words such as energy, entertainment, information, growth, achievement, great, fast, brilliant, talent, vision or more, I am aware of the probability that mania is on the loose and is being rewarded and cultivated, and that the possibility of peacefulness, wisdom and a good life is being further spoiled and neglected. Oh dear, enough of this.

It will be lovely to be back in Curly Flat again and to be with you on that beautiful, special, dark night.

best pre-christmas wishes
yours sincerely,
Vasco Pyjama

P.S. COULD YOU PLEASE ORDER, FROM THE BAKERY, A LARGE CHRISTMAS CAKE FOR THE DUCK.

P.P.S. COULD YOU MAKE THAT EXTRA LARGE, JUST TO BE ON THE SAFE SIDE. THANKS.

Dear Vasco

I'm sorry to hear that you are presently finding the world to be such an unhappy place. Actually, about two thirds of humanity <u>are</u> fairly miserable and will remain so. The problem is that the one third who are contented enough are pretty well invisible. It seems to me that happy souls are inclined to hide or disguise their contentment as a way of protecting and preserving it; so you don't get to see much obvious happiness and you might easily imagine that all the world is depressed. But human happiness exists! It is truly the love that dares not speak its own name. Nothing attracts so much hate and envious attack as simple human happiness. What an appalling fact of life. There is a great cruel ongoing war waged compulsively by the miserable majority against the contented. No wonder happiness lies low! And you will never read about this war in the newspapers — not directly — because it has been going on since time began and it is regarded as the normal and proper state of affairs. Although happiness is greatly outnumbered it has wisdom on its side — and a great keen love of life — and an instinct for survival — and a vision which enables it to see far ahead and behind

and through the darkest night – and an unfailing
ability to recognise its own kind as well as the enemy
which would destroy it. So it survives. Against all
odds it survives – but almost invisibly – <u>the invisible
third</u>! They move about at dawn and in the evening;
on the backroads and byways; they often look almost
drab and you might easily not notice them unless you
are one of them; they lie hidden in the landscape;
they lie in the long grass watching the clouds; they
laze in secluded dells hearing the music of small birds;
they rarely make the news. But you can find them
Vasco, and they can find you; there are ways.
But take good care – this is a very nasty war, this
war against happiness – a primitive, brutal war.
Be brave Vasco –

yours truly

Mr. Curly

x x x

19

Dear Vasco,
I have just remembered something!
Each day is a lifetime.
In the morning we are born.
The day lies before us: vast and bright and new. We say, "Good Morning!" as a prayer and blessing because a good morning may bring a good day and a good life.

By lunchtime we have come to mid-life.
We take a hearty meal and rest. We are
in the midst of the day's demands and we
are doing our plain duty in attending to
them. This is how we find out the truth about
ourselves and the truth about the world.
What a thing to find out! But we have to.

The evening is calm. We sup and reflect. We ready ourselves for the end and prepare for the hereafter: for the next day: a bit of tidying; a little reparation, some shared peace and pleasure and then a prayer on the pillow. An owl hoots. "It was a good life" we say. A cricket sings, the lamp fades and it is over. We die.

So good evening Vasco; good day to you and good morning too!

Yours truly

Mr. Curly

x x x

22

Dear Mr. Curly,

I hope you are well. I'm still wandering far and wide, looking at the world, and now I realise and sort of accept that I am observing and am part of a world which is dying. This is certainly a sad understanding and seems to imply that life is not worth living but, strangely, this is not how I feel. The vital question now seems to be — shall our dear old earth die badly or well? This matters, I think, and seems to be worth working with and struggling with: how do we attend the dying earth? It seems peculiar to be grieving about a death which has not yet occurred and very confusing to mourn ahead of time but this seems a wise and proper thing to learn about because there will be no possibility of a requiem after the event; no fine words or music, and no tears — all those things which can help make sense of death and sweeten it. Perhaps, little by little, we can start doing this already; perhaps a cheerful vase of daffodils can also be, sometimes, a small wreath. We need to be careful with this however — and gentle too because what bothers me most is the feelings of the innocent children. Their hearts are not yet ready for such burdens. So how do we proceed with them? How do we be with them? I must say that when I am amongst them I can only feel that all shall be well and I accept this happiness as a simple pleasure, but when they depart I grow troubled and sad.

How we have wallowed too deeply in the history of man's inhumanity to man — the endless stories of "who did what to whom" and how little we have known or cared or understood about man's cruel persecution of nature, the animals and the earth. Already the holocaust is well in motion and, as with the approaches of of all those other great tragedies and holocausts, — even when the writing is on the

wall – we act as if the worst is not going to
happen. In the light of all this, Curly, I ask
you as I ask myself each morning, " WHAT is
WORTH DOING AND WHAT iS WORTH HAVING ? "
These are big questions and I am curious
about your answers. I look forward to hearing
from you. For the time being I have my
faith and I am doing what I can.
　　　　　Yours cheerfully
　　　　　　　and entirely seriously
　　　　　　　　　Vasco Pyjama
　　　　　　　　　　　x x x

Dear Vasco,

in response to your question "What is worth doing and what is worth having?" I would like to say simply this. It is worth doing nothing and having a rest; in spite of all the difficulty it may cause, you must rest Vasco — otherwise you will become RESTLESS!

I believe the world is sick with exhaustion and dying of restlessness. While it is true that periods of weariness help the spirit to grow, the prolonged, ongoing state of fatigue to which our world seems to be rapidly adapting is ultimately soul destroying as well as earth destroying. The ecology of evil flourishes and love cannot take root in this sad situation. Tiredness is one of our strongest, most noble and instructive feelings. It is an important aspect of our CONSCIENCE and must be heeded or else we will not survive. When you are tired you must HAVE that feeling and you must act upon it sensibly — you MUST rest like the trees and animals do.

Yet tiredness has become a matter of shame! This is a dangerous development. Tiredness has become the most suppressed feeling in the world. Everywhere we see people overcoming their exhaustion and pushing on with intensity — cultivating the great mass mania which all around is making life so hard and ugly — so cruel and meaningless — so utterly graceless — and being congratulated for overcoming it and pushing it deep down inside themselves as if it were a virtue to do this. And of course Vasco, you know what happens when such strong and natural feelings are denied — they turn into the most powerful and bitter poisons with dreadful consequences. We live in a world of these consequences and then wonder why we are so unhappy.

So I gently urge you Vasco, do as we do in Curly Flat — learn to curl up and rest — feel your noble tiredness — learn about it and make a generous place for it in your life and enjoyment will surely follow. I repeat: it's worth doing nothing and having a rest.

yours sleepily,

Mr. Curly xxx

Dear Mr. Curly

the journey is livelier and more enjoyable than ever. I attribute this to the fact that I am losing my grasp of things. How pleasing it is to lose ones grasp!

There is a time to grasp and a time to hold and there has been too much grasping and too little holding in this life.

Holding is of the arms and the breast and the heart. It is steady in its nature and requires commitment. Grasping rhymes with gasping and is essential for certain emergencies. It is a desperate activity of the hands which would much rather be touching, constructing, dismantling, picking flowers, patting animals, scratching the head or stroking the chin. I must say however that in order to hold

something it is sometimes necessary
to grasp it first like a duck, after it
has been spooked by a sinister beast!
 Anyway Curly, I hold something very
dear to me which you said many years ago:
"The bird of paradise does not alight
on the hand that grasps."
 This is a helpful thing to understand
and I thank you for those words.
  And many others too!
   Yours faithfully,
   Vasco Pyjama

Dear Vasco,
swirling season has come to Curly Flat and there
is much much whirling and twirling.

Wish you were here.
Love, Mr. Curly.

Dear Mr. Curly, my heart is heavy with a great sadness. It feels like such an old, old sadness — so full and still and beautiful; so painful. I want to <u>be</u> with it. I want to stay here and become like it.

with love.

Vasco Pyjama

P.S. IT FEELS SO, SORT OF, "WELL ROUNDED" TOO.

32

Dear Vasco,
here's a picture of me preparing to
water ski across Lake Lacuna.
I can only manage one ride a day
and that's in the evening when the
ducks fly home to roost on the
far side of the lake. I walk back
along the shore which looks quite

beautiful in the moonlight and I
often think of you then and wish
you well.

  Good health Vasco!

    Yours truly

      Mr. Curly.

P.S. That's a bread stick the ducks are
  holding in their beaks!

Dear Mr. Curly,
I have done little travelling lately because
I have been so dreadfully weary. Can it
be true as old Ecclesiastes said; that all
things lead to weariness? Surely not. Perhaps
the opposite is true: that all nothings lead
to weariness. I have a peculiar feeling
Curly, that I am worn out from something
I haven't yet done and the more I don't
do it, the more exhausted I become.
How strange. Could it be something I haven't
said? Something I haven't realised?
Perhaps it's something I haven't finished!
It must be very large and true whatever it
is and a lively struggle in the doing
but I look forward to it immensely. I know
I need it. First, however, I must curl up
in my chair and sleep deeply with the duck.

Perhaps I'll dream of this thing and wake up refreshed and do it. My fond wishes to you Mr. Curly, and to all at Curly Flat.

Yours sleepily,

Vasco Pyjama
x x x

P.S. Not having breakfast can make you weary. THAT'S FOR SURE!

Dear Vasco,

how pleased I was to receive your letter.
I trust that by now you have had sleep and
rest enough to return to the enjoyment of your
journey. What an achievement it is to sleep
deeply; and what an achievement also to be
wide awake. I suspect that one leads to the
other. And be careful not to mix them
together too much — keep them separate and
distinct or you'll end up stuck in that
troubled, tragic state of semi-consciousness
into which so much of the world is always
sliding: troubled sleep and trouble waking up:
it cannot live well and it cannot die well.
It just wears itself down. By the way Vasco,
there's an old Curly Flat remedy for
insomnia. In the garden you must dig a hole
as deep as yourself and find a small stone
in the bottom. Then climb out of the

hole, fill it in and go inside to a good, delicious dinner and a glass or two of wine. Then go to bed with the stone under your pillow and lie there listening to it with your eyes closed. Soon you'll be asleep. Apparently it works!

Anyway, I'd better finish now; stay in touch — you'll always find me here.

Warm wishes Vasco and good luck!

yours sincerely Mr. Curly. xxx

P.S. Waking up: Now that's a big subject. Remedies there are many but how many of them actually work?!!!

Dear Mr. Curly,
I am still a little shaken having recently
witnessed, for the first time, something called
a "football match". It was awful. Two opposing
teams of men, with great skill and energy,
thwarted and violated each other, quite obsessively
and shamelessly in full view of a large crowd for
more than one and a half hours.
   Such greed and desperate snatching I have
never seen before; such injury, sadism and
sabotage perpetrated in the cause of advantage
over one's fellows. I saw not the smallest
kindness or act of good faith pass between the
teams. More interestingly, the crowd was
utterly approving of all this trouncing and
hurting and deceiving — in fact it seemed
to thrive on it and became radiant when
the spectacle was most violent.

The questions that occur to me are: why do
people celebrate such primitive greed and
conflict — what _is_ this need? Why do
they desire an unbalanced outcome? What
do they mean when they say " It's just
a game" and why do they need to have
it out there in front of them but well and truly
removed from them — if they love it so much
why aren't they doing it themselves — thwarting
and grabbing and dominating and causing
pain and injury? — maybe they are, but in a

sneaky way, and they feel good to see it all acted out in this big public ritual. Public confession, I'd call it, and I guess that's not a bad thing. Anyway the duck had a terrible day but, as usual, took the spectacle of human madness and sickness in its stride – or should I say,"in its waddle". As we know, ducks don't stride; nor are they strident!
Good wishes dear friend.

   yours truly and in a waddling spirit
         Vasco Pyjama.

Dear Vasco,

autumn has come once more to Curly Flat. The leaves are falling, the days are becoming shorter and certain birds have already departed. In the forest, yesterday evening, I came upon a child crouched over a tiny grave and placing flowers carefully around the little cross made of twigs. I learned from the child that it was a birds grave and when I asked what kind of bird the child, after a long pause, simply replied, "a small, brown bird." I left the child to its devotions and passed on into a darker part of the forest, with all its grandeur and peace, and was there filled suddenly with a great grief and also a great, tender joy and gladness for what I had just seen. Then, a little tearfully, I lay down on the forest floor to contemplate the divinity of children and small brown birds and, so doing,

I fell into a deep and blissful sleep on
a bed of ferns. How I love the forest
Vasco and how radiant is the autumn with
all its dying and going to sleep.
 Warm wishes to yourself and the duck
  Yours truly,
   Mr. Curly

P.S. Such tears and such sleeps are very good
for the complexion, so I'm told!

Dear Mr. Curly,

what a pleasure it was to receive your letter and hear of the beautiful autumn in good old Curly Flat. I haven't got any idea where I am at the moment and don't mind not knowing for I most certainly do not feel at all lost. You will be pleased to know, I'm sure, that my direction-finding duck is in excellent health — feathers as white as an angel and beak all gold and smooth like a good butternut pumpkin. What a duck! The creature seems so enthusiastic and occupied with the business of just being a duck and doesn't appear interested in anything more or anything else. Come to think of it Curly, in all of my travels I never once met a duck which could be called a rich duck or a famous duck — I never met a

religious duck or a fashionable duck or even a republican duck. Funny thing, that. They were always just ducks and quite dignified about it. I suspect they work pretty hard at that and good on them. And good on us as well Mr. Curly. You and me.

Yours sincerely,

Vasco Pyjama x x x

Dear Vasco,

it is the shortest day here in Curly Flat — the winter solstice. We had a very interesting time trying to measure this shortest day. How does one measure a day? Length is one matter but depth and width are just as important. For instance, a short day may be very deep or a long day may be shallow and narrow. What seems to be vital is whether or not the day is spacious, in which case the <u>roundedness</u> of the day is perhaps the most important factor. After all, a round day holds happiness most successfully — happiness itself being of a rounded shape, as you have observed.

The shortest day always reminds me that life is short but no sooner am I conscious of that than I am reminded that life is also very long. This is a most comforting paradox,

for when I know that it is short, life seems
more precious and sweet: I am overcome
with a great sense of forgiveness and my
sufferings seem more bearable and fleeting —
in fact they almost feel like blessings. And
when I know that life is long I am reassured
and contented that the great wheel will
surely turn and natural justice will come to pass
most certainly. But once again Vasco, it is not
the length of life which is important, it is
the shape and the spaciousness-for therein
lies the potential for a beautiful freedom.
It is the roundness of life which matters.
A round life is surely a happy life —
and dare I say — it is a good life.
     Please consider these reflections as
a small picnic of thoughts we may share
together — as we have shared picnics

of sandwiches and wine on the shores of Lake Lacuna in summers past. Those were happy days — and they will come again.

Fare well Vasco!

with salutes and smiles,

Mr. Curly.

Dear Mr. Curly,

I am writing to report a great and wonderful discovery. It is the discovery of my own stupidity and what a marvellous and enjoyable thing it is for me.

As my journey has become lonelier I have somehow grown more stupid in what I feel is a natural and comfortable way. Perhaps it is the fine example set by the duck or perhaps it is because there is nobody to chastise me with strictures or an intelligent gaze — the clever world can be so unforgiving, don't you think; so cruel and oppressive to the stupid part of our nature. Stupidity is like love, in this respect Curly, in that it will find a way and if it is suppressed or thwarted too much it will become a demon and enter surreptitiously into the world as cruelty, coldness or misery. The need to be clever and excellent and brilliant eventually brings a particular kind of weariness and the time comes to let dear old stupidity play its wonky hand. That time has come for me and I think the duck is relieved, as indeed I am.

So I feel, Curly, that I am leaving the vast continent

of solitude and entering the land of stupidity: my promised land and sanctuary of freedom: my lost country of new life and good sleep and forgiveness: my poor, long-suffering, beautiful stupidity — friend of my childhood, I have found you at last and I am coming home.

That's how it seems to me Mr. Curly and I find that I have quite a capacity for slow-wittedness and dumb silliness which seems to suit me down to the ground. I <u>like</u> it. There's almost a spiritual quality in it...! Come to think of it, the paintings I always liked the most were always a bit on the stupid side.

Do you know what I mean Curly?

I'm sure you do.
Yours happily
Vasco Pyjama x xx
P.S. I'm still quite clever too.

Dear Vasco,

I was delighted to receive your letter this morning and read the joyous news that you have finally embraced your stupidity and found such blessed relief. How very good for your heart Vasco. How marvellous! What a momentous achievement this embrace has been; and what a splendiferous liberation awaits you. What glorious songs the birds will now sing for you — great fugues of rapture, just you wait, as the miracle of your "beautiful stupidity" comes wobbling and clanking into your life and sets you free. My most extravagant congratulations Vasco and a warm welcome to the fold.

After I had read your letter I, straight away, seized my tin whistle and went up to the top field where I did a celebratory dance in your honour — a sort of weird jig. This was quite a stupid thing to do because the ground was slippery and muddy from the rain which was pelting down and I kept falling over and made quite a mess of my new corduroy trousers.

Still, I had a lovely bowl of soup for dinner this evening which was all the more delicious for me having fallen in the mud and I've never enjoyed a bowl of soup so much in all my life. It goes to show you, doesn't it. I'd better hop into bed now because I'm feeling very pleasantly sleepy.

The day is done.

Goodnight Vasco,

yours truly,

Mr. Curly

xxx

Dear Vasco,
just a quick note from Curly Flat
to let you know the result of this
year's Ceremony of the Butterfly's Choice.
After much drama and nervous deliberation
on the part of the insect and much gasping
from the crowd, the butterfly finally
settled on the lavender. This, of course.

will be of consequence in the conduct of
courtships, funerals, the teaching of
songs to children and a host of other
ordinary daily matters. The last time
we had a lavender year many chickens
came home to roost and I would welcome
that were it to happen again. It was
a very good year.

I must fly. Yours sincerely

Mr. Curly

Dear Mr. Curly,

no sooner do I graciously accept the huge, rollicking fact of my permanent stupidity and begin to laugh and enjoy it than I am quite suddenly overtaken by an astounding new vision of human madness. The wholeness and perfect clarity of the vision, its majestic, symphonic form is so profoundly moving — so utterly humbling and bracing that my heart, in response, has concocted from the elements of the revelation a strange calm energy - almost a rapture — which no doubt I will need in order to bear the consequences of such an insight.

Many times in the past I have deemed the world mad in a devil-may-care manner. How wise and satisfied I felt to say it like that. But now, and quite significantly I suspect, just as I have committed myself to the acceptance of my ongoing stupidity, I suddenly see the nature of madness as I have never seen it before and I am quite awestruck.

I'm not concerned here with the visible, pitiful madness of the grinning wretch who stands banging his head against a tree or the one who sits naked on a street corner rocking to and fro and weeping mournfully. Compassion can make some sense of this.

Instead I now behold the great, symphonic, invisible madness: the accumulating, collective, interactive madness called normal life: those millions of human lives, deeds and moments which in themselves seem in order but which, by the nature of their relationship, one to the other over time, amount to a massive miserable absurdity: the great undertow of human depravity, malice and wretchedness in which we must somehow conduct our lives. Perhaps I feel something of the awe and humility a lone sailor might feel as he sits in his very tiny boat, in the quiet of a

brewing storm, and beholds all around and
beneath him the great heaving ocean on which
he must stay afloat and hold to his course.
I am a sailor on a sea of madness.
Ahoy there Mr. Curly!
       yours faithfully,

           Vasco Pyjama.

Dear Vasco,

the rose plants have just, this day, been made available at the Curly Flat rose farm. As usual, a small ensemble from the Academy of Ancient Music performed a selection of old airs and dances in celebration. I purchased two roses for my collection: "Baby's Bottom" and "Grandmother's kiss". Like all roses from the farm the origins of these two plants are unknown; they are old "mystery roses" and, of course, the ensemble only played old music of unknown authorship, probably composed by birds in the dawn of history. "Baby's Bottom", as you might imagine, has a plump, rounded flower with pink petals of the most delicate texture and colour. The perfume is delightfully reminiscent of a baby's breath.

"Grandmother's kiss" has a large, blowsy, crinkled flower with an abundance of big loose petals of deep crimson. It has a distinct "handbag" fragrance which comes in great volumes and alters markedly as the day progresses. The evening aroma is quite different to the aroma of the morning.

How arresting is the credential, "unknown origin"! How deep and rich it seems. How

vibrant and free and magical, like a talisman,
seems that creature, that plant or that thing
of "unknown origin".

    Enjoy the sea of madness Vasco. It is the
wildest of the seven seas certainly, but the most
wondrous sailing can be had there. Above you
is the sky of gladness, all so full of ancient
music and babies' breath and birds and
the perfume of roses!

        Good health Vasco.
           yours faithfully

              Mr. Curly.

Dear Vasco,

although spring seems to be arriving cautiously this year in Curly Flat, the doves have started mating with remarkable vigour and conviction. The courtship dances of doves are studied with serious interest in Curly Flat. With careful interpretation these little tangos and flamencos reveal much about the current state of nature and prospects for the coming season. Judging by recent performances I would say that we're in for a summer of "considerable character". I don't recall when I last saw so much ardour combined with such dash and flamboyance. There is an unusually strong sense of glee and purpose in the doves this year and as well as being inspiring and delightful to watch, I think it bodes well generally.

Birds are such good teachers, Vasco, in many things, but particularly in the matters of making music and making love. If we could do these things with as much conviction as they do we would surely fly like them as a simple consequence.

I'll write again soon, but for the moment there's something I want to do in the garden. I must fly. All good wishes dear friend.

Yours truly

Mr. Curly ×××

Dear Vasco,

spring has come once more to Curly Flat and the roses are starting to bloom. How contented I feel as I contemplate the roses. How complete life seems in the presence of these ancient perfumes and petals. How liberated from the desire to "better" myself and how sweetly intoxicated I am by these dear, precious moments of self-acceptance given to me, so generously, by the rose. Around me, in the morning sunshine, the bees hum and various unseen fowls warble old songs concerning the arrival of good, blue eggs. Along the shores of Lake Lacuna, over the water and from the small valleys around Curly Flat I hear the occasional pealing of the life-goes-on bells — simple declarations from

the distance that life is worth living —
a domestic prayer from an unknown household,
rung out in thanksgiving for the morning
now passing and announcing that the
afternoon and its pleasures and duties are
soon to begin ___ or perhaps a chimed
observance that sadness has passed in a
particular home and that relief and
gratitude have begun ___ any of life's
ordinary precious moments being honoured
as they come and go by whoever is taken by
the impulse to do so. How brave and reassuring
are the bells of Curly Flat — bells of
spontaneity; bells of acceptance; bells of joy
and simple duty: life-goes-on bells! Perhaps

you still hear them Vasco, ringing in your
dreams; I hope so.

The sound of a bell and the perfume
of a rose: these things cannot be
improved — they are perfectly complete.
Warmest spring wishes.

Go well vasco
and ding dong!
with love,
Mr. Curly

Dear Vasco,
I've composed a little poem for
you in honour of spring; it's a
tongue twister called "Friends
Like Fronds".

I'm fond of friends like fronds.
I am Quite frondly, I would say.
Friends behave like fronds and fronds
Like friends in every way.

I hope you like it.
    Yours frondly
        Mr. Curly.

Dear Mr. Curly,

Greetings! I hope this message reaches you before December 25th because I want to wish you and the others at Curly Flat a most merry and curly christmas — and a nicely resolved one too. A bit of clarity makes a very lovely Christmas decoration I say!

I won't be home for the big day and feel not a scrap of homesickness about that. Christmas used to disturb me a bit — you know, all that yearning — but not so much any more. I now think that homesickness comes from sick homes — unresolved homes! Anyway Curly, I'm beginning to think that my true home is in heaven and I don't want to go there on christmas day. On the subject of sickness and greetings, I saw a mysterious old inscription above a doorway on my travels recently. I pass it on to you for your contemplation: "better the kiss of a leper than the handshake of a fool." I have pondered much on that and feel it to be important. What do you think?

In closing I will say that, more than ever, I share your love of the christmas music and will be with you in spirit as I sing those carols with the duck beneath beautiful stars on christmas eve. Peace be with you Mr. Curly.

Yours truly,

Vasco Pyjama
xxx

P.S. "The handshake of a foolish leper" - that's a worrying thought!

P.P.S "Clarity begins at home" - that's a good thought!

Dear Vasco Pyjama

It is autumn in Curly Flat. Something vast and marvellous is coming to an end. How perfect and radiant is the death of anything which has run its true course. How beautiful is the death of summer, dear Vasco. Perhaps only that which is true can complete itself.

How this poor world is crowded and poisoned and choked with unfinished business. We must make way for new life! As I write, I hear children in the distance singing sad little eulogies for the fallen leaves. It is late in the afternoon but the sun is shining very brightly. Perhaps this is the best place to finish my letter. Be careful Vasco. Much love — yours sincerely

Mr. Curly

Dear Mr Curly,

it's springtime where I am at present; the sun is shining and the birds are singing beautifully — life is a miracle. There are so many astonishing and wonderful things to talk about. I'll write again soon.

lots of warm wishes,

Vasco.

P.S. A great thing has happened. I've fallen in love.